William Knox, Lizbeth Bullock Humphrey

Oh, Why Should the Spirit of Mortal be Proud?

William Knox, Lizbeth Bullock Humphrey

Oh, Why Should the Spirit of Mortal be Proud?

ISBN/EAN: 9783337345716

Printed in Europe, USA, Canada, Australia, Japan

Cover: Foto ©Thomas Meinert / pixelio.de

More available books at **www.hansebooks.com**

I.

WHY SHOULD THE
SPIRIT OF MORTAL
BE PROUD

OH, WHY SHOULD THE SPIRIT

OF MORTAL BE PROUD?

BY

WILLIAM KNOX

DESIGNS BY MISS L. B. HUMPHREY

Engraved by John Andrew & Son

—⊱≎⊰—

BOSTON

LEE AND SHEPARD, PUBLISHERS

NEW YORK

CHARLES T. DILLINGHAM

1882

JOHN WILSON
& SON.
UNIVERSITY
PRESS.

H, why should the spirit of mortal
be proud?
Like a swift fleeting meteor, a fast-flying cloud,
A flash of the lightning, a break of the wave,
Man passeth from life to his rest in the grave.

The leaves of the oak and the willow shall fade,
Be scattered around and together be laid;
And the young and the old, and the low and the high.
Shall moulder to dust and together shall lie.

HE infant a mother attended and
loved;
The mother that infant's affection who
proved;
The husband that mother and infant
who blessed,
Each, all, are away to their dwellings of rest.

HE maid on whose cheek, on whose
brow, in whose eye,

Shone beauty and pleasure,—her triumphs are by;

And the memory of those who loved her and praised,

Are alike from the minds of the living erased.

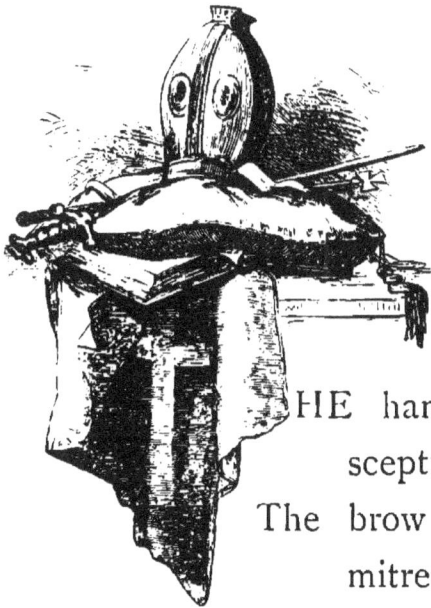

HE hand of the king that the
sceptre hath borne;
The brow of the priest that the
mitre hath worn;
The eye of the sage and the heart of the brave,
Are hidden and lost in the depth of the grave.

HE peasant whose
       lot was to sow and to reap;
The herdsman, who climbed with his goats up
    the steep;
The beggar, who wandered in search of his bread,
Have faded away like the grass that we tread.

HE saint who enjoyed the communion
of heaven,
The sinner who dared to remain unforgiven,
The wise and the foolish, the guilty and just,
Have quietly mingled their bones in the dust.

So the multitude goes, like the flower or the weed
That withers away to let others succeed;
So the multitude comes, even those we behold,
To repeat every tale that has often been told.

FOR we are the same our fathers have
    been ;
We see the same sights our fathers have seen, —
We drink the same stream and view the same
    sun,
And run the same course our fathers have run.

The thoughts we are thinking our fathers would
      think ;
From the death we are shrinking our fathers would
      shrink ;
To the life we are clinging they also would cling ;
But it speeds for us all, like a bird on the wing.

THEY loved, but the story we cannot
    unfold ;
They scorned, but the heart of the haughty
    is cold ;
They grieved, but no wail from their
    slumbers will come ;
They joyed, but the tongue of their gladness is dumb.

They died, ay! they died: and we things that are
      now,
Who walk on the turf that lies over their brow,
Who make in their dwelling a transient abode,
Meet the things that they met on their pilgrimage
      road.

SEA ! hope and despondency, pleasure
     and pain,
  We mingle together in sunshine and
     rain ;
And the smiles and the tears, the song and the
    dirge,
Still follow each other, like surge upon surge.

'T is the wink of an eye, 't is the draught of a breath.
From the blossom of health to the paleness of death,
From the gilded saloon to the bier and the shroud, —
Oh, why should the spirit of mortal be proud?

www.ingramcontent.com/pod-product-compliance
Lightning Source LLC
Chambersburg PA
CBHW021550270326
41930CB00008B/1454